This journal belongs to

_____

66

A great book not only enhances your life experience, but it can also change you.

—OPRAH

Oprah's

THE LIFE YOU WANT

BOOK LOVER'S JOURNAL

HEARST
HOME

READING IS MY ABSOLUTE favorite way to spend time. Reading opens a person up. It exposes you and gives you access to anything your mind can hold. When I learned to read at age 3, I discovered there was a whole world to conquer that went beyond our farm in Mississippi.

Books were a way to escape, but I've since learned they offer so much more: They are memoirs that show us what people are truly capable of, spiritual guides that connect us to the divine, poetry collections that tackle life's eternal questions, histories that make sense of our shared past, roadmaps that take us on a journey to authenticity and, above all, stories that leave us forever transformed.

Now, you know that I love to share the books that have hooked me, starting way back with *The Deep End of the Ocean*, by Jacquelyn Mitchard, the first Oprah's Book Club selection. We've put this journal together to give you a place to capture the books that you've loved, as well as the sentences that stopped you in your tracks and the titles you want to read next. It has prompts to help you remember old favorites and new recommendations—novels, memoirs, nonfiction, poetry, short story collections, book club picks—and plenty of space for notes.

As you fill out the pages, I hope this will become a collection of the authors you've loved, the books you didn't know you needed, and lessons you've learned about the world and your place in it.

Oprah

For book reviews and to learn of Oprah's next Book Club selections, visit **OprahDaily.com**, and follow us @ **@Oprahsbookclub**

Contents

Life-transforming ideas have always come to me through books.

—BELL HOOKS

Books That Made a Difference

The prompts in this section will help you recall the books that moved you, changed you, inspired you. You don't need to fill out all of these entries right away. Maybe you haven't come across a memorable memoir or a love story for the ages... *yet*. When you do, return to these pages.

MY FAVORITE BOOK OF ALL TIME

Title: _____

_____

Author: _____

Why I loved it:

_____

_____

_____

_____

_____

_____

The time in my life when I read it:

_____

_____

_____

_____

_____

_____

"I've talked a lot about how much *Beloved* meant to me. I believe Toni Morrison was our conscience. Our seer. Our truth-teller. She was a magician with language, who understood the power of words. She used them to roil us, to wake us, to educate us, and help us grapple with our deepest wounds. Nowhere more than in *Beloved*."

—OPRAH

The quotes I always remember:

_____

_____

_____

_____

_____

_____

_____

_____

_____

_____

_____

_____

_____

_____

_____

_____

THE BOOK THAT REMINDS ME OF THE BEAUTY IN THE ORDINARY

Title: _____

_____

Author: _____

Details the author noted that I never would have:

_____

_____

_____

_____

_____

_____

_____

_____

_____

_____

_____

_____

Details I've begun to see in my own life:

_____

_____

_____

_____

_____

_____

_____

_____

What those tiny things mean to me:

_____

_____

_____

_____

_____

_____

_____

_____

THE FIRST BOOK THAT
MADE ME FEEL SEEN

Title: _____

_____

Author: _____

What resonated most with me:

_____

_____

_____

_____

_____

_____

The scene I continue to think about:

_____

_____

_____

_____

_____

_____

"Maya Angelou's autobiography *I Know Why the Caged Bird Sings* was the first book I ever read that made me feel my life as a 'colored girl' growing up in Mississippi deserved validation. I loved it from the opening line: 'What you looking at me for? I didn't come to stay...' "

—OPRAH

Quotes that hit home:

_____

_____

_____

_____

_____

_____

_____

_____

The truest part of the book:

_____

_____

_____

_____

_____

_____

_____

THE BEST BOOK I RECEIVED AS A GIFT

Title: _____

_____

Author: _____

Why it was such a good gift:

_____

_____

_____

_____

_____

_____

What did it mean that it came from that person:

_____

_____

_____

_____

_____

_____

> "*A Gentleman in Moscow* was published within days of my
> 20th anniversary. To celebrate, my wife gave me the first edition of
> Tolstoy's *War and Peace* to be published in English (in 1886)."
> —AMOR TOWLES

How seen did I feel when I read it?

_____

_____

_____

_____

_____

_____

_____

Where is my copy now?

_____

_____

_____

_____

_____

_____

_____

THE BEST BOOK I GAVE AS A GIFT

Title: _____

_____

Author: _____

Why _I_ liked it so much:

_____

_____

_____

_____

_____

_____

Why I liked it so much for other people:

_____

_____

_____

_____

_____

> "I still remember the shock of recognition I felt when, in 1982, I first read Alice Walker's just-published *The Color Purple*. I went into the bookstore and bought every copy they had. I would just stop somebody and say, 'Excuse me, excuse me, sir. Have you read *The Color Purple*?'"
> —OPRAH

My favorite response from someone I gave it to:

_____

_____

_____

_____

_____

_____

_____

The next person I'll share it with:

_____

_____

_____

_____

_____

_____

_____

THE LAST BOOK THAT SURPRISED ME

Title: _____

_____

Author: _____

What surprised me most:

_____

_____

_____

_____

_____

_____

Why that was interesting:

_____

_____

_____

_____

_____

_____

"I love to be surprised. I don't steer
clear of anything, as long as it's interesting."
—EDWIDGE DANTICAT

What I'll take from the experience of having my expectations upended:

_____

_____

_____

_____

_____

_____

_____

_____

The quote that jumped out:

_____

_____

_____

_____

_____

_____

_____

_____

THE NOVEL THAT HIT ME HARD

Title: _____

_____

Why it struck a chord:

_____

_____

_____

_____

_____

_____

_____

The moment that was most powerful:

_____

_____

_____

_____

_____

_____

_____

> *"The Water Dancer*, by Ta-Nehisi Coates, is an incredible book—as beautiful as it is tragic. I knew early on the book was going to cut me up. I ended up with my soul pierced."
> —OPRAH

The quotes I'll always remember:

_____

_____

_____

_____

_____

_____

_____

_____

_____

_____

_____

_____

_____

_____

_____

_____

_____

_____

THE BOOK THAT REMINDS ME NOT TO JUDGE

Title: _____

_____

Author: _____

The judgment I didn't know I was holding:

_____

_____

_____

_____

_____

_____

The uncomfortable truth that it brought up:

_____

_____

_____

_____

_____

_____

> "Henry James refuses to allow the reader to make easy judgments...his insisting on nuance, half-light, and suggestion...his deep understanding of the strangeness and the wavering nature of motive and feeling in human relationships."
> —COLM TÓIBÍN

The quote that brought me up short:

_____

_____

_____

_____

_____

_____

_____

The reminder I'll take going forward:

_____

_____

_____

_____

_____

_____

_____

THE SELF-HELP BOOK THAT WAS A REVELATION

Title: _____

_____

Author: _____

What surprised me most about this book:

_____
_____
_____
_____
_____
_____

How it helped me live differently:

_____
_____
_____
_____
_____
_____

"I'd never recommended a book in the spiritual or self-help genre before, but because *A New Earth*, by Eckhart Tolle, had such a profound impact on me, I thought others might also be struck by the idea of putting the ego in check and becoming more aware of being rather than doing."

—OPRAH

The advice I'll take with me:

_____

_____

_____

_____

_____

_____

_____

_____

_____

_____

_____

_____

_____

_____

_____

_____

A LOVE STORY FOR THE AGES

Title: _____

_____

Author: _____

Why this love story is above all others:

_____

_____

_____

_____

_____

_____

_____

_____

_____

_____

_____

_____

_____

_____

_____

_____

"Zora Neale Hurston's classic *Their Eyes Were Watching God* is my favorite love story of all time. Janie Mae Crawford spends almost two decades with abusive, domineering men but eventually finds true love with Tea Cake. In the time they have together, he teaches her to open her heart to the world."
—OPRAH

The quotes that I'll never forget:

_____

_____

_____

_____

_____

_____

_____

_____

_____

_____

_____

_____

_____

_____

_____

_____

THE BOOK I GO BACK TO

Title: _____

_____

Author: _____

Why I return to it:

_____

_____

_____

_____

_____

_____

_____

_____

_____

_____

_____

_____

_____

_____

> "I rarely read novels again. But I read *The Bluest Eye*
> every few years and still feel altered every time
> by the character Pecola Breedlove and Toni Morrison's
> adept portrayal of life in this community."
> —OPRAH

What I got from it the first time I read it:

_____

_____

_____

_____

_____

_____

_____

What I got from it this time:

_____

_____

_____

_____

_____

_____

_____

_____

A MEMORABLE MEMOIR

Title: _____

_____

Author: _____

Why I loved their story:

_____

_____

_____

_____

_____

_____

_____

The quote I loved:

_____

_____

_____

_____

_____

_____

"There are so many lessons to be learned from *Finding Me*, a breathtaking memoir about triumphing over adversity and trauma. Viola Davis leaves it all on the page—from her beginnings in South Carolina as the fifth of six children born in a sharecropper's shack to acclaim as an actor, producer, and philanthropist. I was so moved by this book that I just had to share it with the entire Oprah's Book Club audience."
—OPRAH

The most profound life truth:

_____

_____

_____

_____

_____

_____

_____

_____

_____

_____

_____

_____

_____

_____

"

Reading for the pure
pleasure of it, for the beautiful
stillness that surrounds you
when you hear an author's words
reverberating in your head.

—PAUL AUSTER

A COMING OF AGE...THAT KEEPS COMING BACK TO MIND

Title: _____

_____

Author: _____

When I read it:

_____

_____

_____

_____

The reason I love it:

_____

_____

_____

_____

_____

_____

_____

"Page after page of reading *White Oleander*, by Janet Fitch, I fell in love with a story that deeply moved me and vivid passages that described the sky as the color of peaches and compared sorrow to the taste of a copper penny."
—OPRAH

The quote that took my breath away:

_____

_____

_____

_____

_____

_____

_____

What was different about this story of transformation:

_____

_____

_____

_____

_____

_____

_____

_____

THE BOOK THAT LIGHTENS ANY DAY

Title: _____

_____

Author: _____

The reason it's just so good:

_____

_____

_____

_____

_____

_____

The quote that never fails to make me laugh:

_____

_____

_____

_____

_____

_____

The scene I go back to:

_____

_____

_____

_____

_____

_____

_____

_____

_____

_____

The friend who might like to read it next:

_____

_____

_____

_____

_____

_____

FAVORITE COOKBOOK

Title: _____

Author: _____

Why I loved it:

_____

_____

_____

_____

_____

_____

_____

_____

_____

_____

_____

_____

_____

_____

My favorite recipes:

_____

_____

_____

_____

_____

_____

_____

_____

_____

_____

Notes:

_____

_____

_____

_____

_____

_____

_____

THE COFFEE TABLE BOOK TO LONG FOR

Title: _____

Author: _____

What it's about:

_____

_____

_____

_____

_____

_____

The best inspiration from it:

_____

_____

_____

_____

_____

_____

> "I so enjoy thumbing through the pages of *The Way We Live,*
> by Stafford Cliff—it's like being on a train, passing other people's
> houses, and getting to see a small minute of how they live."
> —OPRAH

Why it's so beautiful to me:

_____

_____

_____

_____

_____

_____

_____

_____

Who might I give this to:

_____

_____

_____

_____

_____

_____

_____

THE BOOK THAT INTRODUCED ME TO ANOTHER WORLD

Title: _____

_____

Author: _____

Where it was set:

_____

_____

_____

_____

_____

What I loved most about that world:

_____

_____

_____

_____

_____

_____

_____

What it showed me that I hadn't seen before:

_____

_____

_____

_____

_____

_____

_____

How it affected how I see my part of the world:

_____

_____

_____

_____

_____

_____

_____

A BOOK THAT CHANGED MY MIND

Title: _____

_____

Author: _____

What it's about:

_____

_____

_____

_____

_____

_____

What I used to think:

_____

_____

_____

_____

_____

_____

> "Lucy Corin's debut story collection, *The Entire Predicament*, jolted me into an entirely fresh way of seeing the familiar. Imagine suddenly seeing in ultraviolet."
> —KAREN RUSSELL

What I think now:

_____

_____

_____

_____

_____

_____

_____

The thing that shifted my opinion:

_____

_____

_____

_____

_____

_____

_____

THE BOOK THAT HELPED ME FIGURE OUT WHERE I BELONG

Title: _____

_____

Author: _____

What it helped me see about the place I was:

_____

_____

_____

_____

_____

_____

How it helped me choose something more:

_____

_____

_____

_____

_____

> *"Long Island,* by Colm Tóibín, is a novel about a woman's reckoning with infidelity, with long-lost love, with secrets, and the universal struggle we all have to figure out where we truly belong."
>
> —OPRAH

A quote I'll always remember:

_____

_____

_____

_____

_____

_____

_____

_____

Why I'm grateful for it:

_____

_____

_____

_____

_____

_____

_____

_____

THE BOOK THAT'S A GREAT ESCAPE

Title: _____

_____

Author: _____

Why it's perfect for moments when I'm burned out:

_____

_____

_____

_____

_____

_____

Why it helps turn my brain off:

_____

_____

_____

_____

_____

_____

> "When the world is too much, I love to read thrillers and romance novels. I just want to lose myself in something either intriguing or ludicrously romantic."
> —ROXANE GAY

A scene that was distracting in just the right way:

_____

_____

_____

_____

_____

_____

_____

The elements that I'll look for in other books when I need an escape:

_____

_____

_____

_____

_____

_____

_____

_____

THE BOOK THAT IS A HEART-HEALER

Title: _____

_____

Author: _____

Why it struck a chord:

_____
_____
_____
_____
_____
_____

The aspect that felt most restorative:

_____
_____
_____
_____
_____
_____

> *"The Darkest Child* by Delores Phillips…is a heartbreaker—
> there has never been a more problematic mother-daughter
> relationship in all of literature. But it's also a heart-healer."
> **—TAYARI JONES**

The scene that was most powerful:

_____

_____

_____

_____

_____

_____

_____

_____

The quote that captured the opportunity for growth best:

_____

_____

_____

_____

_____

_____

_____

_____

Reading is a conversation.

—ALBERTO MANGUEL

THE BOOK I WISH I'D READ SOONER

Title: _____

_____

Author: _____

When I read it:

_____

_____

_____

_____

_____

_____

Why the time wasn't right:

_____

_____

_____

_____

_____

_____

> "I wish I'd come to Eric Butterworth's *Discover the Power Within You* sooner, because it expanded and enhanced my view of religion. God isn't 'up there,' he writes, 'the greatest mistake is in believing that we are "only human"…. We are human in expression but divine in creation and limitless in potentiality.'"
> —OPRAH

When would have been better:

_____

_____

_____

_____

_____

_____

_____

_____

What I would've gained:

_____

_____

_____

_____

_____

_____

_____

_____

THE BOOK I WISH
I'D READ LATER

Title: _____

_____

Author: _____

When I read it:

_____

_____

_____

_____

_____

_____

Why the time wasn't right:

_____

_____

_____

_____

_____

_____

"Love in the Time of Cholera, by Gabriel García Márquez—
sorry, but only in your fifth decade will you have experienced enough
heartbreak to truly grasp this great love story."
—ABRAHAM VERGHESE

When would have been better:

_____
_____
_____
_____
_____
_____
_____
_____

What I would've gained:

_____
_____
_____
_____
_____
_____
_____
_____

THE BOOK I'M SURPRISED I HAVEN'T READ YET

Title: _____

_____

Author: _____

The reason I think it's a book for me:

_____

_____

_____

_____

_____

_____

The reason I haven't yet gotten to it:

_____

_____

_____

_____

_____

_____

> "I am working my way through Proust because it seems
> that there is the notion that every writer ought to and because I have
> been a Francophile since my first French class in third grade."
> —ISABEL WILKERSON

When I hope to find the time (or mental space) for it:

_____

_____

_____

_____

_____

_____

_____

What I hope to gain from it:

_____

_____

_____

_____

_____

_____

_____

THE BOOK THAT THRILLED ME

Title: _____

_____

Author: _____

Why it thrilled me so much:

_____

_____

_____

_____

_____

_____

How that feeling is different from being satisfied by a book:

_____

_____

_____

_____

_____

_____

> "*The Waterworks*, by E.L. Doctorow, is one of the most
> thrilling books I've ever read. And I still believe in that, you know?
> That stories should sometimes thrill people."
> —TA-NEHISI COATES

A scene I'll never forget:

_____

_____

_____

_____

_____

_____

_____

A quote I want to remember:

_____

_____

_____

_____

_____

_____

_____

THE BOOK THAT FLIRTS WITH THE SUPERNATURAL

Title: _____

_____

Author: _____

The most bewitching part of this book like its aspect of magic realism or sci-fi or something else:

_____

_____

_____

_____

_____

_____

_____

_____

_____

_____

_____

_____

_____

_____

> "These kinds of books nudge me to remember
> our world is but one facet of an enormous continuity."
> —TRACY K. SMITH

The effect was most captivating because:

_____

_____

_____

_____

_____

_____

_____

What it reminded me about our world:

_____

_____

_____

_____

_____

_____

_____

THE BOOK THAT INSPIRED ME TO BE BETTER

Title: _____

_____

Author: _____

Where I was falling short of the person I want to be:

_____
_____
_____
_____
_____
_____
_____
_____
_____
_____
_____
_____
_____
_____

> "The poetry of Hayden Carruth deserves a lot more attention than it gets—it never fails to speak to me and alter my mindset for the better."
> —GEORGE SAUNDERS

How it reminded me to improve:

_____

_____

_____

_____

_____

_____

_____

A passage that was particularly inspiring:

_____

_____

_____

_____

_____

_____

_____

THE BOOK I CAN'T STOP THINKING ABOUT

Title: _____

_____

Author: _____

Why I'm sure (or not sure) I liked the book:

_____

_____

_____

_____

_____

_____

_____

_____

_____

_____

_____

_____

_____

_____

"The characters in Richard Russo's *Bridge of Sighs* have stayed with me. And the store, the store, the store—almost a central character itself! Russo is so good at capturing these people's lives and community— and so profound on relationships and the meaning of life."

—OPRAH

What I keep thinking about:

_____

_____

_____

_____

_____

_____

_____

_____

The feelings I have:

_____

_____

_____

_____

_____

_____

_____

_____

_____

THE BOOK THAT EXPLAINS THE TIMES WE LIVE IN

Title: _____

_____

Author: _____

The startling similarities between the book and life now:

_____

_____

_____

_____

_____

_____

_____

_____

_____

_____

_____

_____

_____

_____

> "I recently picked up *Dawn* by Octavia E. Butler, and I was stunned by how relevant the themes of the book are to today. She artfully exposes our human impulse to self-destruct."
> —LUPITA NYONG'O

The context it provides:

_____

_____

_____

_____

_____

_____

_____

_____

How I feel about the moment now and the future coming:

_____

_____

_____

_____

_____

_____

_____

THE BOOK THAT ALWAYS MAKES ME CRY

Title: _____

_____

Author: _____

Why it's such a tearjerker:

_____

_____

_____

_____

_____

_____

Why that's just so good:

_____

_____

_____

_____

_____

_____

> "My most memorable book-related weeping occurred early in Cormac McCarthy's *The Road*. I was eating ribs in Chelsea, in Dallas BBQ. I'd just become a father, and something in the book about the dad trying to save his kid from nutso hillbillies—great, here I go again."
> —COLSON WHITEHEAD

The most heartbreaking moment:

_____

_____

_____

_____

_____

_____

_____

The most breathtaking quote:

_____

_____

_____

_____

_____

_____

_____

"

Reading becomes my escape and joy.

—TIYA MILES

THE BOOK THAT MADE ME FEEL LESS ALONE

Title: _____

_____

Author: _____

The thing I thought no one else understood:

_____

_____

_____

_____

_____

_____

The moment in the book I realized someone _did_ understand:

_____

_____

_____

_____

_____

_____

> "Oh so many [authors made me feel less alone]—Iris Murdoch, Chekhov, Zoë Heller, J.D. Salinger—any writer who can reflect us back to ourselves and help us discover who we are."
> —JUDI DENCH

The quote that gave such comfort:

_____

_____

_____

_____

_____

_____

_____

_____

The person I know who might need this too:

_____

_____

_____

_____

_____

_____

_____

_____

THE *OLD* CLASSIC I LOVE

Title: _____

_____

Author: _____

Why it struck a chord:

_____

_____

_____

_____

_____

_____

_____

The character I'll always remember and why:

_____

_____

_____

_____

_____

_____

"The Grapes of Wrath is one of my favorite books. I found it an eye-opening experience traveling with the Joads, enduring their hunger and hardships. Nelson Mandela once told me that of the many books he read in prison that was one of the most important: 'When I closed that book, I was a different man. It enriched my powers of thinking and discipline, and my relationships.' And I've never forgotten that."

—OPRAH

The quote I'll always remember:

_____

_____

_____

_____

_____

_____

_____

_____

A lesson I'll take from this book:

_____

_____

_____

_____

_____

_____

_____

THE *NEW* CLASSIC I LOVE

Title: _____

_____

Author: _____

Why it struck a chord:

_____

_____

_____

_____

_____

_____

_____

The character I'll always remember and why:

_____

_____

_____

_____

_____

_____

"The Story of Edgar Sawtelle, by David Wroblewski, is so engaging, so gripping, so epic that I wanted absolutely everybody to share the joy of this novel. (And if you love dogs, that's a plus.)"
—OPRAH

The quotes I'll always remember:

_____

_____

_____

_____

_____

_____

_____

_____

A lesson I'll take from this book:

_____

_____

_____

_____

_____

_____

_____

_____

THE BOOK THAT SHOWED ME THE POWER OF HERITAGE

Title: _____

_____

Author: _____

What legacy means in the book:

_____

_____

_____

_____

_____

_____

What legacy means in my life:

_____

_____

_____

_____

_____

> "What *Cane River* by Lalita Tademy did is open the door for a lot of people who want to trace their own roots— what that legacy has meant for them."
>
> —OPRAH

The questions I have about my own heritage:

_____

_____

_____

_____

_____

_____

_____

The quote that hit close to home:

_____

_____

_____

_____

_____

_____

_____

THE BOOK THAT REALLY CAPTURED WHAT GRIEF FEELS LIKE

Title: _____

_____

Author: _____

The type of grief the book explored:

_____

_____

_____

_____

_____

The grief that I have suffered:

_____

_____

_____

_____

_____

_____

> "Grief eases just a little when the words match the feelings."
> —MARGARET RENKL

The facet it got so right:

_____

_____

_____

_____

_____

The feeling I had reading such an accurate description:

_____

_____

_____

_____

_____

The comfort it offered:

_____

_____

_____

_____

THE BOOK THAT REMINDED ME OF WHAT MATTERS MOST

Title: _____

_____

Author: _____

The valuable lesson it showed me:

_____

_____

_____

_____

_____

_____

_____

_____

_____

_____

_____

_____

_____

> "I think books with spiritual themes simply point to the deeper mysteries of life—to what lies beyond us, to what's hidden inside of us, or perhaps to an understanding of what truly matters— *The Poisonwood Bible*, by Barbara Kingsolver, affected me that way."
> —SUE MONK KIDD

The importance of remembering this:

_____

_____

_____

_____

_____

_____

_____

_____

The quote I loved about this:

_____

_____

_____

_____

_____

_____

_____

_____

THE BOOK THAT MADE ME WHO I AM TODAY

Title: _____

_____

Author: _____

The trait in myself that I trace to this book:

_____

_____

_____

_____

_____

_____

The way I'd describe myself before:

_____

_____

_____

_____

_____

> "The first writer to show me that there were
> monsters in the world, and that they could be defeated
> (to paraphrase Chesterton), was Stephen King."
> —ALYSSA COLE

The way I'd describe myself after:

_____

_____

_____

_____

_____

_____

_____

_____

The lines I don't want to forget:

_____

_____

_____

_____

_____

_____

_____

_____

THE MOST IMPORTANT BOOK ANYONE SHOULD READ

Title: _____

_____

Author: _____

What it's about:

_____

_____

_____

_____

_____

_____

Why it's so compelling:

_____

_____

_____

_____

_____

_____

"Caste, by Isabel Wilkerson, is an essential read for anyone who cares to really understand the current state of America. It explains where we are, in terms of inequality and racial injustice. I sent this book to 500 people in leadership positions—from senators and mayors to heads of universities—hoping if everyone read it and spread the word, we might save ourselves."

—OPRAH

Who should read it now, and why:

_____

_____

_____

_____

Quote I loved:

_____

_____

_____

_____

_____

_____

_____

_____

_____

_____

66

I'm alone, with what the book and I have to offer each other.

—MARGO JEFFERSON

My Reading Journey

In this section, you can keep track of the books you've read—starting with the ones that inspire a lot of thoughts. Beyond those pages, you'll find Short Takes, a space to capture other reads you don't want to forget.

BOOK NOTES

Use these pages to capture your thoughts on the novels, memoirs, nonfiction, poetry, short story collections, book club picks—in short, all the books that made you think, wowed you, or won't let you go.

Title: _____

Author: _____

When and where I read the book: _____

The kind of book (novel, memoir, poetry, graphic novel, etc.): _____

_____

The plot in one sentence: _____

_____

What I liked best about the book:

_____

_____

_____

_____

A reason the book resonated at this moment in my life:

_____

_____

_____

_____

_____

How I see the world (or myself) differently having read this book?

_____

_____

_____

_____

_____

Quotes I loved from the book:

_____

_____

_____

_____

_____

_____

_____

_____

_____

_____

_____

_____

_____

BOOK NOTES

Title: _____

Author: _____

When and where I read the book: _____

The kind of book (novel, memoir, poetry, graphic novel, etc.): _____
_____

The plot in one sentence: _____
_____

What I liked best about the book:

_____

_____

_____

_____

_____

A reason the book resonated at this moment in my life:

_____

_____

_____

_____

_____

How I see the world (or myself) differently having read this book?

_____

_____

_____

_____

_____

Quotes I loved from the book:

_____

_____

_____

_____

_____

_____

_____

_____

_____

_____

_____

_____

_____

_____

_____

BOOK NOTES

Title: _____

Author: _____

When and where I read the book: _____

The kind of book (novel, memoir, poetry, graphic novel, etc.): _____

_____

The plot in one sentence: _____

_____

What I liked best about the book:

_____

_____

_____

_____

_____

A reason the book resonated at this moment in my life:

_____

_____

_____

_____

_____

How I see the world (or myself) differently having read this book?

_____

_____

_____

_____

_____

Quotes I loved from the book:

_____

_____

_____

_____

_____

_____

_____

_____

_____

_____

_____

_____

_____

_____

BOOK NOTES

Title: _____

Author: _____

When and where I read the book: _____

The kind of book (novel, memoir, poetry, graphic novel, etc.): _____

_____

The plot in one sentence: _____

_____

What I liked best about the book:

_____

_____

_____

_____

_____

A reason the book resonated at this moment in my life:

_____

_____

_____

_____

_____

How I see the world (or myself) differently having read this book?

_____

_____

_____

_____

_____

Quotes I loved from the book:

_____

_____

_____

_____

_____

_____

_____

_____

_____

_____

_____

_____

_____

_____

BOOK NOTES

Title: _____

Author: _____

When and where I read the book: _____

The kind of book (novel, memoir, poetry, graphic novel, etc.): _____

_____

The plot in one sentence: _____

_____

What I liked best about the book:

_____

_____

_____

_____

_____

A reason the book resonated at this moment in my life:

_____

_____

_____

_____

_____

How I see the world (or myself) differently having read this book?

_____

_____

_____

_____

_____

Quotes I loved from the book:

_____

_____

_____

_____

_____

_____

_____

_____

_____

_____

_____

_____

_____

_____

BOOK NOTES

Title: _____

Author: _____

When and where I read the book: _____

The kind of book (novel, memoir, poetry, graphic novel, etc.): _____

_____

The plot in one sentence: _____

_____

What I liked best about the book:

_____

_____

_____

_____

_____

A reason the book resonated at this moment in my life:

_____

_____

_____

_____

_____

How I see the world (or myself) differently having read this book?

_____

_____

_____

_____

_____

Quotes I loved from the book:

_____

_____

_____

_____

_____

_____

_____

_____

_____

_____

_____

_____

_____

_____

BOOK NOTES

Title: _____

Author: _____

When and where I read the book: _____

The kind of book (novel, memoir, poetry, graphic novel, etc.): _____
_____

The plot in one sentence: _____
_____

What I liked best about the book:

_____

_____

_____

_____

_____

A reason the book resonated at this moment in my life:

_____

_____

_____

_____

_____

How I see the world (or myself) differently having read this book?

_____

_____

_____

_____

_____

Quotes I loved from the book:

_____

_____

_____

_____

_____

_____

_____

_____

_____

_____

_____

_____

_____

_____

BOOK NOTES

Title: _____

Author: _____

When and where I read the book: _____

The kind of book (novel, memoir, poetry, graphic novel, etc.): _____

_____

The plot in one sentence: _____

_____

What I liked best about the book:

_____

_____

_____

_____

_____

A reason the book resonated at this moment in my life:

_____

_____

_____

_____

_____

How I see the world (or myself) differently having read this book?

_____

_____

_____

_____

_____

Quotes I loved from the book:

_____

_____

_____

_____

_____

_____

_____

_____

_____

_____

_____

_____

_____

66

We read books to find out who we are.

—URSULA K. LE GUIN

BOOK NOTES

Title: _____

Author: _____

When and where I read the book: _____

The kind of book (novel, memoir, poetry, graphic novel, etc.): _____

_____

The plot in one sentence: _____

_____

What I liked best about the book:

_____

_____

_____

_____

_____

A reason the book resonated at this moment in my life:

_____

_____

_____

_____

How I see the world (or myself) differently having read this book?

_____

_____

_____

_____

_____

Quotes I loved from the book:

_____

_____

_____

_____

_____

_____

_____

_____

_____

_____

_____

_____

_____

_____

BOOK NOTES

Title: _____

Author: _____

When and where I read the book: _____

The kind of book (novel, memoir, poetry, graphic novel, etc.): _____

_____

The plot in one sentence: _____

_____

What I liked best about the book:

_____

_____

_____

_____

_____

A reason the book resonated at this moment in my life:

_____

_____

_____

_____

_____

How I see the world (or myself) differently having read this book?

_____

_____

_____

_____

_____

Quotes I loved from the book:

_____

_____

_____

_____

_____

_____

_____

_____

_____

_____

_____

_____

_____

BOOK NOTES

Title: _____

Author: _____

When and where I read the book: _____

The kind of book (novel, memoir, poetry, graphic novel, etc.): _____
_____

The plot in one sentence: _____
_____

What I liked best about the book:

_____
_____
_____
_____
_____

A reason the book resonated at this moment in my life:

_____
_____
_____
_____
_____

How I see the world (or myself) differently having read this book?

_____

_____

_____

_____

_____

Quotes I loved from the book:

_____

_____

_____

_____

_____

_____

_____

_____

_____

_____

_____

_____

_____

_____

BOOK NOTES

Title: _____

Author: _____

When and where I read the book: _____

The kind of book (novel, memoir, poetry, graphic novel, etc.): _____
_____

The plot in one sentence: _____
_____

What I liked best about the book:
_____
_____
_____
_____
_____

A reason the book resonated at this moment in my life:
_____
_____
_____
_____
_____

How I see the world (or myself) differently having read this book?

_____

_____

_____

_____

_____

Quotes I loved from the book:

_____

_____

_____

_____

_____

_____

_____

_____

_____

_____

_____

_____

BOOK NOTES

Title: _____

Author: _____

When and where I read the book: _____

The kind of book (novel, memoir, poetry, graphic novel, etc.): _____
_____

The plot in one sentence: _____
_____

What I liked best about the book:

_____

_____

_____

_____

_____

A reason the book resonated at this moment in my life:

_____

_____

_____

_____

_____

How I see the world (or myself) differently having read this book?

_____

_____

_____

_____

_____

Quotes I loved from the book:

_____

_____

_____

_____

_____

_____

_____

_____

_____

_____

_____

_____

_____

_____

BOOK NOTES

Title: _____

Author: _____

When and where I read the book: _____

The kind of book (novel, memoir, poetry, graphic novel, etc.): _____

_____

The plot in one sentence: _____

_____

What I liked best about the book:

_____

_____

_____

_____

_____

A reason the book resonated at this moment in my life:

_____

_____

_____

_____

_____

How I see the world (or myself) differently having read this book?

_____

_____

_____

_____

_____

Quotes I loved from the book:

_____

_____

_____

_____

_____

_____

_____

_____

_____

_____

_____

_____

_____

_____

BOOK NOTES

Title: _____

Author: _____

When and where I read the book: _____

The kind of book (novel, memoir, poetry, graphic novel, etc.): _____
_____

The plot in one sentence: _____
_____

What I liked best about the book:
_____
_____
_____
_____
_____

A reason the book resonated at this moment in my life:
_____
_____
_____
_____
_____

How I see the world (or myself) differently having read this book?

Quotes I loved from the book:

BOOK NOTES

Title: _____

Author: _____

When and where I read the book: _____

The kind of book (novel, memoir, poetry, graphic novel, etc.): _____
_____

The plot in one sentence: _____
_____

What I liked best about the book:
_____
_____
_____
_____
_____

A reason the book resonated at this moment in my life:
_____
_____
_____
_____
_____

How I see the world (or myself) differently having read this book?

_____

_____

_____

_____

_____

Quotes I loved from the book:

_____

_____

_____

_____

_____

_____

_____

_____

_____

_____

_____

_____

_____

_____

> **She read books as one would breathe air, to fill up and live.**
>
> —ANNIE DILLARD

BOOK NOTES

Title: _____

Author: _____

When and where I read the book: _____

The kind of book (novel, memoir, poetry, graphic novel, etc.): _____

_____

The plot in one sentence: _____

_____

What I liked best about the book:

_____

_____

_____

_____

_____

A reason the book resonated at this moment in my life:

_____

_____

_____

_____

_____

How I see the world (or myself) differently having read this book?

_____

_____

_____

_____

_____

Quotes I loved from the book:

_____

_____

_____

_____

_____

_____

_____

_____

_____

_____

_____

_____

_____

_____

BOOK NOTES

Title: _____

Author: _____

When and where I read the book: _____

The kind of book (novel, memoir, poetry, graphic novel, etc.): _____
_____

The plot in one sentence: _____
_____

What I liked best about the book:

_____
_____
_____
_____
_____

A reason the book resonated at this moment in my life:

_____
_____
_____
_____
_____

How I see the world (or myself) differently having read this book?

_____

_____

_____

_____

_____

Quotes I loved from the book:

_____

_____

_____

_____

_____

_____

_____

_____

_____

_____

_____

_____

_____

_____

BOOK NOTES

Title: _____

Author: _____

When and where I read the book: _____

The kind of book (novel, memoir, poetry, graphic novel, etc.): _____
_____

The plot in one sentence: _____
_____

What I liked best about the book:

_____

_____

_____

_____

_____

A reason the book resonated at this moment in my life:

_____

_____

_____

_____

_____

How I see the world (or myself) differently having read this book?

_____

_____

_____

_____

_____

Quotes I loved from the book:

_____

_____

_____

_____

_____

_____

_____

_____

_____

_____

_____

_____

_____

BOOK NOTES

Title: _____

Author: _____

When and where I read the book: _____

The kind of book (novel, memoir, poetry, graphic novel, etc.): _____
_____

The plot in one sentence: _____
_____

What I liked best about the book:

_____
_____
_____
_____
_____

A reason the book resonated at this moment in my life:

_____
_____
_____
_____
_____

How I see the world (or myself) differently having read this book?

_____

_____

_____

_____

_____

Quotes I loved from the book:

_____

_____

_____

_____

_____

_____

_____

_____

_____

_____

_____

_____

_____

BOOK NOTES

Title: _____

Author: _____

When and where I read the book: _____

The kind of book (novel, memoir, poetry, graphic novel, etc.): _____

_____

The plot in one sentence: _____

_____

What I liked best about the book:

_____

_____

_____

_____

_____

A reason the book resonated at this moment in my life:

_____

_____

_____

_____

_____

How I see the world (or myself) differently having read this book?

_____

_____

_____

_____

_____

Quotes I loved from the book:

_____

_____

_____

_____

_____

_____

_____

_____

_____

_____

_____

_____

_____

BOOK NOTES

Title: _____

Author: _____

When and where I read the book: _____

The kind of book (novel, memoir, poetry, graphic novel, etc.): _____
_____

The plot in one sentence: _____
_____

What I liked best about the book:

_____

_____

_____

_____

_____

A reason the book resonated at this moment in my life:

_____

_____

_____

_____

_____

How I see the world (or myself) differently having read this book?

_____

_____

_____

_____

_____

Quotes I loved from the book:

_____

_____

_____

_____

_____

_____

_____

_____

_____

_____

_____

_____

_____

BOOK NOTES

Title: _____

Author: _____

When and where I read the book: _____

The kind of book (novel, memoir, poetry, graphic novel, etc.): _____

_____

The plot in one sentence: _____

_____

What I liked best about the book:

_____

_____

_____

_____

_____

A reason the book resonated at this moment in my life:

_____

_____

_____

_____

_____

How I see the world (or myself) differently having read this book?

_____

_____

_____

_____

_____

Quotes I loved from the book:

_____

_____

_____

_____

_____

_____

_____

_____

_____

_____

_____

_____

_____

_____

BOOK NOTES

Title: _____

Author: _____

When and where I read the book: _____

The kind of book (novel, memoir, poetry, graphic novel, etc.): _____

_____

The plot in one sentence: _____

_____

What I liked best about the book:

_____

_____

_____

_____

_____

A reason the book resonated at this moment in my life:

_____

_____

_____

_____

_____

How I see the world (or myself) differently having read this book?

_____

_____

_____

_____

_____

Quotes I loved from the book:

_____

_____

_____

_____

_____

_____

_____

_____

_____

_____

_____

_____

_____

_____

_____

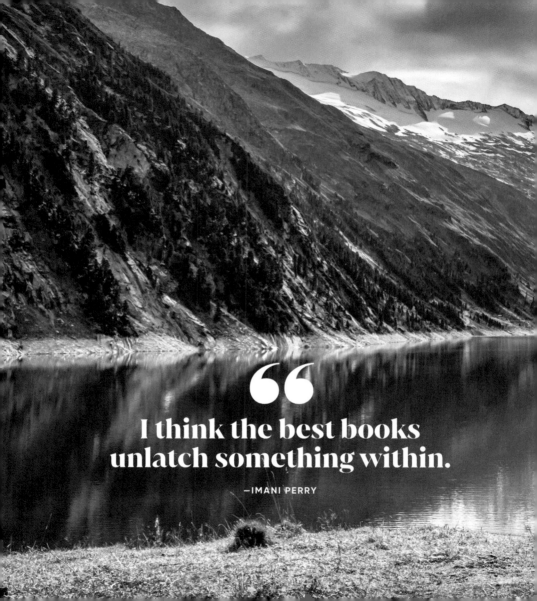

**I think the best books
unlatch something within.**

—IMANI PERRY

SHORT TAKES

Use these pages for other books that were delightful, too good to put down, or the perfect way to while away a few hours.

Title: _____

Author: _____

One sentence that describes it: _____
_____

A line that inspired me: _____
_____
_____
_____
_____

Title: _____

Author: _____

One sentence that describes it: _____
_____

A line that inspired me: _____
_____
_____
_____

Title: _____

Author: _____

One sentence that describes it: _____
_____

A line that inspired me: _____
_____
_____

Title: _____

Author: _____

One sentence that describes it: _____
_____

A line that inspired me: _____
_____
_____

Title: _____

Author: _____

One sentence that describes it: _____
_____

A line that inspired me: _____
_____
_____

SHORT TAKES

Title: _____

Author: _____

One sentence that describes it: _____
_____

A line that inspired me: _____
_____
_____

Title: _____

Author: _____

One sentence that describes it: _____
_____

A line that inspired me: _____
_____
_____

Title: _____

Author: _____

One sentence that describes it: _____
_____

A line that inspired me: _____
_____
_____

Title: _____

Author: _____

One sentence that describes it: _____
_____

A line that inspired me: _____
_____
_____

Title: _____

Author: _____

One sentence that describes it: _____
_____

A line that inspired me: _____
_____
_____

Title: _____

Author: _____

One sentence that describes it: _____
_____

A line that inspired me: _____
_____
_____

SHORT TAKES

Title: _____

Author: _____

One sentence that describes it: _____

_____

A line that inspired me: _____

_____

_____

Title: _____

Author: _____

One sentence that describes it: _____

_____

A line that inspired me: _____

_____

_____

Title: _____

Author: _____

One sentence that describes it: _____

_____

A line that inspired me: _____

_____

_____

Title: _____

Author: _____

One sentence that describes it: _____

_____

A line that inspired me: _____

_____

_____

Title: _____

Author: _____

One sentence that describes it: _____

_____

A line that inspired me: _____

_____

_____

Title: _____

Author: _____

One sentence that describes it: _____

_____

A line that inspired me: _____

_____

_____

SHORT TAKES

Title: _____

Author: _____

One sentence that describes it: _____

_____

A line that inspired me: _____

_____

_____

Title: _____

Author: _____

One sentence that describes it: _____

_____

A line that inspired me: _____

_____

_____

Title: _____

Author: _____

One sentence that describes it: _____

_____

A line that inspired me: _____

_____

_____

Title: _____

Author: _____

One sentence that describes it: _____
_____

A line that inspired me: _____
_____
_____

Title: _____

Author: _____

One sentence that describes it: _____
_____

A line that inspired me: _____
_____
_____

Title: _____

Author: _____

One sentence that describes it: _____
_____

A line that inspired me: _____
_____
_____

SHORT TAKES

Title: _____

Author: _____

One sentence that describes it: _____

_____

A line that inspired me: _____

_____

_____

Title: _____

Author: _____

One sentence that describes it: _____

_____

A line that inspired me: _____

_____

_____

Title: _____

Author: _____

One sentence that describes it: _____

_____

A line that inspired me: _____

_____

_____

Title: _____

Author: _____

One sentence that describes it: _____
_____

A line that inspired me: _____
_____
_____

Title: _____

Author: _____

One sentence that describes it: _____
_____

A line that inspired me: _____
_____
_____

Title: _____

Author: _____

One sentence that describes it: _____
_____

A line that inspired me: _____
_____
_____

SHORT TAKES

Title: _____

Author: _____

One sentence that describes it: _____

_____

A line that inspired me: _____

_____

_____

Title: _____

Author: _____

One sentence that describes it: _____

_____

A line that inspired me: _____

_____

_____

Title: _____

Author: _____

One sentence that describes it: _____

_____

A line that inspired me: _____

_____

_____

Title: _____

Author: _____

One sentence that describes it: _____

_____

A line that inspired me: _____

_____

_____

Title: _____

Author: _____

One sentence that describes it: _____

_____

A line that inspired me: _____

_____

_____

Title: _____

Author: _____

One sentence that describes it: _____

_____

A line that inspired me: _____

_____

_____

SHORT TAKES

Title: _____

Author: _____

One sentence that describes it: _____

A line that inspired me: _____

_____

_____

Title: _____

Author: _____

One sentence that describes it: _____

A line that inspired me: _____

_____

_____

Title: _____

Author: _____

One sentence that describes it: _____

A line that inspired me: _____

_____

_____

Title: _____

Author: _____

One sentence that describes it: _____
_____

A line that inspired me: _____
_____
_____

Title: _____

Author: _____

One sentence that describes it: _____
_____

A line that inspired me: _____
_____
_____

Title: _____

Author: _____

One sentence that describes it: _____
_____

A line that inspired me: _____
_____
_____

SHORT TAKES

Title: _____

Author: _____

One sentence that describes it: _____

_____

A line that inspired me: _____

_____

_____

Title: _____

Author: _____

One sentence that describes it: _____

_____

A line that inspired me: _____

_____

_____

Title: _____

Author: _____

One sentence that describes it: _____

_____

A line that inspired me: _____

_____

_____

Title: _____

Author: _____

One sentence that describes it: _____
_____

A line that inspired me: _____
_____
_____

Title: _____

Author: _____

One sentence that describes it: _____
_____

A line that inspired me: _____
_____
_____

Title: _____

Author: _____

One sentence that describes it: _____
_____

A line that inspired me: _____
_____
_____

SHORT TAKES

Title: _____

Author: _____

One sentence that describes it: _____

_____

A line that inspired me: _____

_____

_____

Title: _____

Author: _____

One sentence that describes it: _____

_____

A line that inspired me: _____

_____

_____

Title: _____

Author: _____

One sentence that describes it: _____

_____

A line that inspired me: _____

_____

_____

Title: _____

Author: _____

One sentence that describes it: _____
_____

A line that inspired me: _____
_____
_____

Title: _____

Author: _____

One sentence that describes it: _____
_____

A line that inspired me: _____
_____
_____

Title: _____

Author: _____

One sentence that describes it: _____
_____

A line that inspired me: _____
_____
_____

SHORT TAKES

Title: _____

Author: _____

One sentence that describes it: _____

_____

A line that inspired me: _____

_____

_____

Title: _____

Author: _____

One sentence that describes it: _____

_____

A line that inspired me: _____

_____

_____

Title: _____

Author: _____

One sentence that describes it: _____

_____

A line that inspired me: _____

_____

_____

Title: _____

Author: _____

One sentence that describes it: _____
_____

A line that inspired me: _____
_____
_____

Title: _____

Author: _____

One sentence that describes it: _____
_____

A line that inspired me: _____
_____
_____

Title: _____

Author: _____

One sentence that describes it: _____
_____

A line that inspired me: _____
_____
_____

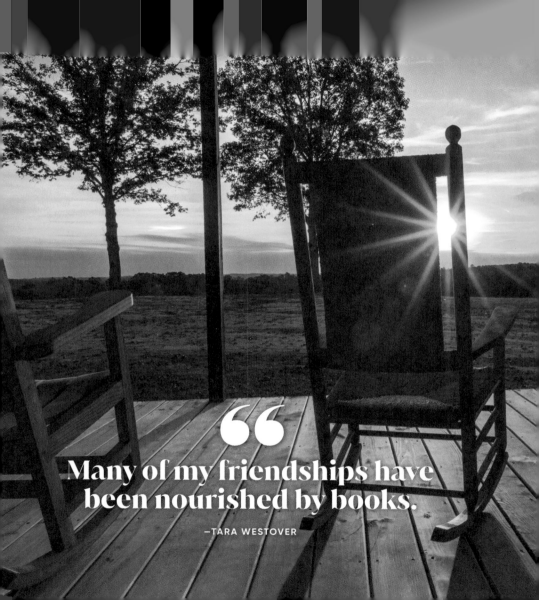

Many of my friendships have been nourished by books.

—TARA WESTOVER

Reading Together

Reading over one hundred books together? I don't think I ever imagined that, way back in 1996 when the book club launched, but what a wonderful experience it's been so far!

Whether you're part of a book club now or gearing up to start one with friends, these pages are meant to help you make the most of your time with one another. Who knows? Maybe you'll find inspiration for your next group meeting (or solo read!) among my Oprah's Book Club picks.

ADVICE FOR LAUNCHING YOUR OWN

Oprah's Book Club

Some book clubs are forever. Here's how yours can stay the course.

It seems easy enough to start a book club—choose a book, invite a few friends, add cocktails and carbohydrates. But turns out, the "keeping it going" part can be a challenge, even for the most dedicated reading groups. That's where these guidelines can come in handy...

WHEN CHOOSING A BOOK, MAKE SURE AT LEAST ONE PERSON IN THE CLUB HAS ALREADY READ IT.
This is helpful for a few reasons: One, it means that you have someone who can lead the discussion that month. For another, it means at least one member thinks your group will have enough to talk about. What it doesn't mean is that everyone will like the book—but that's okay. A robust conversation can clarify what each of you did (or did not) find important/meaningful/

transcendent. The back-and-forth might even change your mind.

CHANGE UP YOUR BOOK SELECTIONS.
If you pick a long novel, like *Familiaris* by David Wroblewski or *The Covenant of Water* by Abraham Verghese, you might want to pick a shorter read for your next meeting so that people don't feel overwhelmed. If your book club has been going strong for a few years, you might mix genres to keep conversations fresh— choose a memoir, a collection of poetry, a self-help book—or pick something that's just been translated or re-released.

DON'T FREAK OUT ABOUT THE FOOD.
A home-cooked meal inspired by the setting of the month's choice sounds terrific. But what's

also delicious? Carry out. As writer and longtime book club host Liesl Schillinger says, "It's book club, not gourmet club."

THAT SAID, IT'S ALSO NOT FIGHT CLUB.

Robust discussion is wonderful—and as mentioned, a spirited debate might even shift someone's initial assessment. But groups begin to splinter when a critique of a book... tips into criticism of a person or their opinion. If you're inclined to take the contrarian view, by all means do. Just be mindful to express your thoughts kindly. (And if the group picks what you think is a truly dreadful selection? Feel free to skip that month's meeting.)

RESPECT THE CALENDAR.

To keep momentum, you'll want to meet every six to eight weeks, but you'll likely want to wrap up your book club year in early November, because no matter how many good intentions, no one will be able to meet amid the annual steeplechase that is Thanksgiving to New Year's.

OFFER LIFETIME MEMBERSHIPS.

Some folks will have to drop out—they move to another city, the arrival of triplets, winning Powerball. You'll have to replace them, of course, and new people with new opinions often revitalize a group. But be fluid: Some of those "new" members might leave and some originals may drift back, which delivers a different boost.

CONSIDER ASKING THE AUTHOR TO DROP IN.

Jean Hanff Korelitz, author of *The Plot*, started a company, BooktheWriter.com, to connect book clubs with book authors. She says many writers are happy to Zoom into a night's conversation or stop by if it's a local gathering. It's polite to offer payment and cover expenses if it's in person and, of course, show support by purchasing the book. Inviting the author is a unique way to celebrate your first, 10th, or 20th book club anniversary.

FUN FACTS

TOTAL NUMBER OF PAGES READ:
42,350
(give or take a foreign edition)

BOOKS WRITTEN BY A DEBUT AUTHOR:
25

AVERAGE NUMBER OF BOOKS AN AUTHOR PUBLISHED BEFORE THEIR BOOK CLUB SELECTION:
3.7

BOOKS MADE INTO AN HBO MINISERIES:
1
I Know This Much Is True
by Wally Lamb

BOOKS MADE INTO MOVIES:
35

NUMBER OF BOOKS, 1996 TO 2024:
109

BOOKS ORIGINALLY WRITTEN IN ANOTHER LANGUAGE:
7

OPRAH EDITION COPIES SOLD IN THE FIRST 15 YEARS OF THE BOOK CLUB:
OVER 55 MILLION

BESTSELLING PICK OF ALL TIME:
A Tale of Two Cities
BY CHARLES DICKENS
(200 million copies sold, minus a few undocumented 19th-century sales)

BOOKS THAT TAKE PLACE IN CALIFORNIA, NEW YORK, OR WISCONSIN:
23

BOOKS WRITTEN AFTER THE AUTHOR'S 60TH BIRTHDAY:
17

BOOKS TRANSLATED BY THE AUTHOR'S SPOUSE:
1
Night
by Elie Wiesel

BOOKS IN WHICH WOMEN—WHO AREN'T NUNS!—TAKE UP RESIDENCE IN A CONVENT: 2
Paradise by Toni Morrison
The Pilot's Wife by Anita Shreve

**Books can be
sacred objects.**

— JAYNE ANNE PHILLIPS

"

Books are knowledge. Books are reflection. Books change your mind.

—TONI MORRISON

MEMOIRS:
12

AUTHORS WHO HAVE RECEIVED HONORARY KNIGHTHOODS FROM THE QUEEN OF ENGLAND:
2
(Elie Wiesel and Sidney Poitier)

AUTHORS WHO HAD THEIR WORK PRESERVED IN THE NATIONAL MILLENNIUM TIME CAPSULE (TO BE OPENED IN 2100):
4
(Maya Angelou, Toni Morrison, Ernest J. Gaines, and William Faulkner)

NATIONAL BOOK AWARDS–WINNING AUTHORS:
10

AUTHORS WHO HAVE WON AN OSCAR:
2
(Sidney Poitier and Viola Davis)

AUTHORS PICKED MORE THAN ONCE:
13

THE BOOK THAT MADE OPRAH SAY: "WHEN I READ IT, IT FELT LIKE COMING HOME":
The Love Songs of W.E.B. Du Bois
by Honorée Fanonne Jeffers

BOOKS THAT ARE 400 OR MORE PAGES:
38

BOOKS THAT MADE GAYLE SAY, "OPRAH, JUST TELL ME WHAT'S GOING TO HAPPEN NEXT—I'M AFRAID TO TURN THE PAGE":
1
The Water Dancer
by Ta-Nehisi Coates

BOOKS THAT OPRAH CONSIDERS "REQUIRED READING FOR ALL HUMANITY":
2
Night
by Elie Wiesel
AND
Caste
by Isabel Wilkerson

NOVELS:
89

OPRAH'S BOOK CLUB LIST

Family Dramas

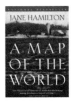

A Map of the World
BY JANE HAMILTON

In this harrowing story, the lives of the Goodwin family permanently change after they witness their neighbor's daughter drown in a pool, an event that leads to the downfall of a family once at peace.

A Million Little Pieces
BY JAMES FREY

Frey's memoir supposedly recounted three months he spent in jail, but it was revealed he lied about major plot details. Five years after, Oprah and the author sat down again for a far-reaching conversation that ended on the gift of figuring out the truth of who we are and a way to honor that.

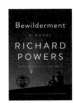

Bewilderment
BY RICHARD POWERS

This intimate novel, from a Pulitzer Prize–winning author, is about astrobiologist Theo Byrne, who is raising his 9-year-old son after his wife's death. Tender and timely, the story covers existential questions about the place of humans in the world.

Cane River
BY LALITA TADEMY

The author walked away from a job in Silicon Valley to write the stories of slave-born women in this multigenerational family saga. Oprah said the story opens the door for people who want to trace their own roots and look at what that legacy has meant for them.

Fall on Your Knees
BY ANN-MARIE MACDONALD

This Canadian novelist weaves a fascinating story of the Piper family, across a mystically charged journey spanning five generations of one family's sin, guilt, and redemption.

Freedom
BY JONATHAN FRANZEN

This saga centers on a seemingly picture-perfect family in Minnesota. But we quickly learn that the old trope is true: Looks are indeed deceiving.

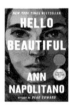

Hello Beautiful
BY ANN NAPOLITANO

Written in homage to the classic *Little Women*, this book follows the story of the four Padovano sisters. Their close-knit, rambunctious family is forever changed when the eldest, Julia, marries.

I Know This Much Is True
BY WALLY LAMB

This frank book takes an honest look at mental illness, domestic abuse, and family dysfunction with a refreshing touch of humor.

River, Cross My Heart
BY BREENA CLARKE

Illustrating the Black experience in America, this book follows Alice and Willie Bynum, a couple whose lives completely change after the death of their 5-year-old daughter.

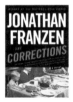

The Corrections
BY JONATHAN FRANZEN

This is a grandly entertaining novel for the new century — a comic, tragic masterpiece about a family breaking down in an age of easy fixes. Richly realistic, darkly hilarious, and deeply humane.

The Covenant of Water
BY ABRAHAM VERGHESE

Verghese introduces the fictional Big Ammachi, matriarch of a Christian family in Kerala, India, and follows three generations from 1900 to 1977, transporting readers across time and continents.

The Deep End of the Ocean
BY JACQUELYN MITCHARD

In 1996, Oprah's first-ever selection was this suspenseful novel, which follows a family as they learn to cope—through humor and unrelenting strength—with the disappearance of a child.

The Love Songs of W.E.B. Du Bois
BY HONORÉE FANONNE JEFFERS

Epic doesn't begin to describe this tour-de-force of a novel, which touches on family, legacy, identity, and America's tangled roots. Ailey, our protagonist, is the second of three girls, who grows up visiting her mom's family in a small town in Georgia, and becomes curious about her heritage. Her first-person narration is a coming-of-age story meets history. But Jeffers also incorporates a sweeping narrative about Ailey's ancestors.

The Story of Edgar Sawtelle
BY DAVID WROBLEWSKI

Edgar Sawtelle, who was born mute, has only ever known a peaceful, bucolic life on his parents' farm—until a trauma threatens to change that. Oprah called it "so engaging, so gripping, so epic." Sixteen years later, she chose **Familiaris,** an immense novel that tells the origins of that first story. Its 975 pages are laced with magic, history, philosophy, whimsy, and humor.

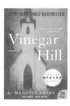

Vinegar Hill
BY A. MANETTE ANSAY

Ellen Grier must move in with her in-laws, raise two children, and deal with her husband's unemployment in a startling portrayal of life in the country gone awry.

We Were the Mulvaneys
BY JOYCE CAROL OATES

A hopeful if haunting depiction of a family in crisis, this novel explores the after-effects of a tragedy, and how they can reverberate over the years, on siblings and parents alike.

Memoirs

Becoming
BY MICHELLE OBAMA

"This is Michelle Obama's story, of course," said Oprah, "but I know it's going to spark within you the desire to think about your own becoming."

Finding Me
BY VIOLA DAVIS

In her powerful and empowering memoir, the third Black woman to earn the so-called "EGOT," Davis leaves it all on the page.

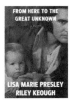

From Here to the Great Unknown
BY LISA MARIE PRESLEY AND RILEY KEOUGH

This captures the life of Elvis's daughter—told through recordings she left and the help of her own daughter, Riley Keough, who hoped the book would "cut through the judgment to the core of who Lisa Marie Presley was."

Love Warrior
BY GLENNON DOYLE

"Whether you're married or single, whether you're a mom or not," Oprah said, "all women are going to see themselves in these pages. It's daring, and it's raw, and it's filled with a lot of naked—I do mean naked—truths!"

Night
BY ELIE WIESEL

Written by Nobel Prize winner and Holocaust survivor Wiesel, "*Night* should be required reading for all humanity," Oprah said.

Stolen Lives
BY MALIKA OUFKIR AND MICHÈLE FITOUSSI

A story of privilege, tumult, and endurance: Born the daughter of a general and adopted by the King of Morocco when she was 5, Malika Oufkir and her family were then imprisoned for 24 years.

That Bird Has My Wings
BY JARVIS JAY MASTERS

Masters has been incarcerated since 1981. "His story, of a young boy victimized by addiction, poverty, violence, the foster care system, and later the justice system, profoundly touched me then, and still does today," said Oprah.

The Heart of a Woman
BY MAYA ANGELOU

In this autobiography, Angelou describes moving to New York with her son, Guy, and describes a community of Black artists that molded her.

The Many Lives of Mama Love
BY LARA LOVE HARDIN

In this memoir of "lying, stealing, writing, and healing," Hardin recounts how opioid addiction destroyed her quiet suburban life—and how she built something stronger out of the rubble.

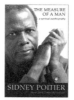

The Measure of a Man
BY SIDNEY POITIER

"An exercise in self-questing" is what Poitier called his memoir. "I wanted to find out, as I looked back at a long and complicated life, how well I've done at measuring up to the values I myself have set." A breathtaking read.

The Sun Does Shine
BY ANTHONY RAY HINTON

This memoir reads like an epic novel. Hinton was falsely convicted of murder and spent 30 years on death row before he was finally released.

Wild
BY CHERYL STRAYED

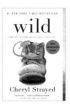

This impactful memoir follows a lost young woman on a quest to self-discovery as she travels through the Pacific Crest Trail, learning to cope with her mother's death and a severed marriage.

> "Many people, myself among them, feel better at the mere sight of a book."
>
> —JANE SMILEY

The Many Facets of Love

An American Marriage
BY TAYARI JONES

This novel redefines the traditional American love story. The reader finds themselves inside a world that many don't know about but impacts us all.

A Virtuous Woman
BY KAYE GIBBONS

Gibbons will make you fall in love with Blinking Jack Stokes and Ruby Pitt Woodrow, an unexpected pair that find solace in their differences.

Behold the Dreamers
BY IMBOLO MBUE

Tracing the intersection of an immigrant couple and the husband and wife who employ them, this novel examines race and class, the economy, and immigration.

Daughter of Fortune
BY ISABEL ALLENDE

A love story, Allende's title is centered on Eliza Sommers, an orphan raised in Chile who eventually creates a new life for herself during the 19th-century California gold rush.

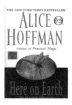

Here on Earth
BY ALICE HOFFMAN

In this novel, March Murray returns to her Massachusetts hometown to face her past, including a man she was previously in love with.

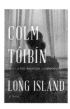

Long Island
BY COLM TÓIBÍN

Although it follows the characters from his novel *Brooklyn*, this novel has everything you need to know in its own completely riveting story about a woman's reckoning with the universal struggle we all have: to figure out where we truly belong.

Ruby
BY CYNTHIA BOND

This finely wrought love story explores what happens when a woman needs to face her childhood demons in the face of racial injustice.

The Twelve Tribes of Hattie
BY AYANA MATHIS

Depicting one family's journey from the segregated South through five and a half turbulent, soul-searing decades, this masterful debut focuses on the matriarch of a Black family navigating love and loss through the Great Migration.

Wellness
BY NATHAN HILL

A hilarious and tender exploration of love, marriage, life hacks, technology, and how to reconcile the people we once were with the strangers we inevitably, eventually, become.

Journeys

American Dirt: A Novel
BY JEANINE CUMMINS

It's clear that we need to have a different kind of conversation about *American Dirt*," Oprah said, after this pick generated comments about who can tell which stories. She brought together people from all sides to talk about who gets to publish what stories, while noting, "I appreciated that book—it helped me to see immigrants and the whole migration process differently than I had before."

Let Us Descend
BY JESMYN WARD

This riveting novel tells the story of Annis, a young, enslaved woman, separated from her mother and sold in the South. "A fan of her writing for years," Oprah calls this newest offering "a vital work for our culture."

The Poisonwood Bible
BY BARBARA KINGSOLVER

The Price family, led by their evangelical Baptist father Nathan, begins to unravel as their bond and faith is tested during a mission to Africa.

The Road
BY CORMAC MCCARTHY

An unnamed man and his young son journey through a post-apocalyptic world where only glimmers of humanity exist: "It is so extraordinary. I promise you," Oprah said.

The Sweetness of Water
BY NATHAN HARRIS

Set at the very end of the Civil War, Harris's powerful first novel centers on two brothers, who are at last leaving the plantation where they've spent their entire lives, and grappling with what will come next.

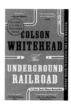

The Underground Railroad
BY COLSON WHITEHEAD

"Every now and then, a book comes along that reaches the marrow of your bones," said Oprah. "This is the one. It's a tour de force, and I don't say that lightly." This harrowing tale of a runaway teenage slave has supernatural elements that only heighten its power.

The Water Dancer
BY TA-NEHISI COATES

This odyssey follows the story of Hiram Walker, a young man born as a slave on a plantation in Virginia who has been gifted a mysterious, magical power that eventually saves his life when he nearly drowns in a river. "I have not felt this way about a book since *Beloved*," Oprah said.

Self-Help

A New Earth
BY ECKHART TOLLE

Tolle believes that we as a people are ready to undergo a profound transformation—to transcend ego in favor of a higher form of consciousness.

Bittersweet
BY SUSAN CAIN

A nonfiction title that explores how we deal with sadness. "This book," said Oprah, "has the power to transform the way you see your life and even the world."

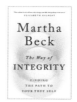

The Way of Integrity
BY MARTHA BECK

Filled with aha moments and practical exercises, this is for anyone seeking a road map on the journey to truth.

Life in Community

A Fine Balance
BY ROHINTON MISTRY
Four main characters share a cramped apartment in India in the 1970s. Mistry has been compared to Dickens in his finest years—so profoundly able to look at the human spirit juxtaposed against inhumane conditions.

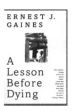

A Lesson Before Dying
BY ERNEST J. GAINES
Gaines's novel details what happens after Jefferson, a Black man, is the only survivor of a shooting that left one white store owner killed.

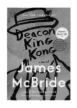

Deacon King Kong
BY JAMES MCBRIDE
A 19-year-old drug dealer with an incredible pitching arm. A death-defying drunkard. A mobster with a soft side. These are just a sampling of the characters in this soaring novel set in the projects of 1969 Brooklyn.

Demon Copperhead
BY BARBARA KINGSOLVER
The author re-envisions the Charles Dickens classic *David Copperfield*, setting it in modern-day Appalachia to counter some of the condescension and downright snobbery directed at the region in which she was born and still lives.

Gilead, Home, Lila, and Jack BY MARILYNNE ROBINSON
Oprah chose four books by the same author at the same time—the Pulitzer Prize-winning Marilynne Robinson. All take place in "a fictional Iowa town. A quartet of masterpieces," said Oprah.

> "When I read, I like to go somewhere else in my mind with stories that touch our real world without taking place in it.

—TOMI ADEYEMI

House of Sand and Fog
BY ANDRE DUBUS III
Combining unadorned realism with profound empathy, this explores the lives of three people attempting to live the American Dream—and what happens when it all goes awry.

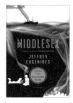

Middlesex
BY JEFFREY EUGENIDES
Told from narrator Calliope Stephanides's perspective, this novel explores the complexities of growing up female but struggling between male and female identity and her Greek and American heritage.

Mother of Pearl
BY MELINDA HAYNES
Set in 1950s Mississippi, the book touches on racism and lives intertwined in a small-town in the South.

Olive, Again
BY ELIZABETH STROUT
Oprah fell in love with this prickly protagonist "despite her flaws." (The book is Strout's follow-up to her 2008 Pulitzer Prize–winning book *Olive Kitteridge*.) In 2024, Oprah selected **Tell Me Everything,** which revisits the characters inhabiting her many novels and the small town of Crosby, Maine.

Paradise
BY TONI MORRISON
From the town's ancestral origins in 1890 to the fateful day of an assault, *Paradise* tells the story of a people ever mindful of the relationship between their spectacular history and a void "where random and organized evil erupted when and where it chose."

Say You're One of Them
BY UWEM AKPAN
A collection of short stories told through the eyes of children living in Africa, this collection is both distressing and masterful.

Small Things Like These
BY CLAIRE KEEGAN
This luminous short novel follows a young father struggling with the darker truths in his Irish village during Christmas. It's a holiday tale that exemplifies small acts of courage.

Song of Solomon
BY TONI MORRISON
Morrison explores the life of Macon Dead Jr., a.k.a. Milkman, the son of the richest Black family in a small town, as he grows in and out of the South. It's a novel expressing passion, tenderness, and a magnificence of language.

Historical

Stones from the River
BY URSULA HEGI
The main character, Trudi Montag, grapples with Nazism in Germany while learning that despite her difference in appearance as a dwarf, all humans are unique.

The Invention of Wings
BY SUE MONK KIDD
Set in the early 1800s, this novel centers on an abolitionist from Charleston, South Carolina, her sister, and their slave, who all share a desire to be free.

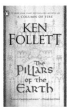

The Pillars of the Earth **BY KEN FOLLETT**
Though it's a hefty read at 800 pages, Oprah swears that this 12th-century story (with the erection of a Gothic cathedral at the center) is one you won't be able to put down.

The Reader
BY BERNHARD SCHLINK

Set in postwar Germany, *The Reader* zeroes in on the relationship between Michael Berg and Hanna, a woman twice his age who ends up on trial for a reckless crime. A nuanced love story and a parable of German guilt and atonement, it's unforgettable in its psychological complexity and stylistic restraint.

> "Good books
> are not completed
> until they are
> read by a reader,
> and each
> reader completes
> the book in
> a different way."
>
> —ALAN LIGHTMAN

Cultural Historical

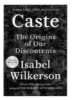

Caste
BY ISABEL WILKERSON

"Of all the books I've chosen for the book club over the decades, there isn't another that is more essential a read than this one," Oprah said of this book that traces a caste system in the U.S.

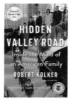

Hidden Valley Road
BY ROBERT KOLKER

An engrossing true story that reads like a medical detective journey, this introduces the Galvin family, who had six children diagnosed with schizophrenia—and six children untouched by the illness. They became science's great hope in the quest to understand—and even cure—the disease.

Coming of Age

Back Roads
BY TAWNI O'DELL

A dark portrayal of boyhood, Back Roads follows 19-year-old Harley Altmyer, the son of a woman jailed for murdering his father (a serial abuser).

Black and Blue
BY ANNA QUINDLEN

A woman runs away from her abusive husband to begin anew and give her son a better life.

Breath, Eyes, Memory BY EDWIDGE DANTICAT

Weaving political upheaval into the narrative, novelist Danticat explores the life of 12-year-old Sophie Caco, a girl forced to move to New York to live with a mother who's had little involvement in her upbringing.

Ellen Foster
BY KAYE GIBBONS

Against all odds, 11-year-old Ellen never gives up her belief that there is a place for her in the world, a home which will satisfy all her longing for love, acceptance, and order.

Icy Sparks
BY GWYN HYMAN RUBIO

This beautifully written first novel revolves around Icy Sparks, a girl finding herself in eastern Kentucky in the 1950s— an unforgettable heroine in the tradition of Scout in *To Kill a Mockingbird*.

Nightcrawling
BY LEILA MOTTLEY

Mottley began her astonishing debut novel when she was just 16. The result, about a young woman in Oakland, her brother, and the 9-year-old next door, has received raves.

She's Come Undone
BY WALLY LAMB

Lamb's novel chronicles the life of Dolores Price, a 13-year-old who welcomes womanhood and is eventually dead set on conquering her insecurities.

The Bluest Eye
BY TONI MORRISON

A celebrated work of fiction—and Toni Morrison's first novel—follows 11-year-old Pecola Breedlove as she grows into herself in the author's hometown of Lorain, Ohio.

The Rapture of Canaan
BY SHERI REYNOLDS

After becoming pregnant, 14-year-old Ninah fears the reaction of her grandfather, the leader of a strict Christian congregation.

Where the Heart Is
BY BILLIE LETTS

At 17, and seven months pregnant, Novalle Nation journeys across the country, only to get stranded in Oklahoma with little cash and less hope. A funny, candid depiction of girlhood, it puts a human face on the look-alike trailer parks and malls of America's small towns. It will make you believe in the strength of friendship, the goodness of down-to-earth people, and the healing power of love.

White Oleander
BY JANET FITCH

In this story, we see a young woman—who bounces between foster homes after being separated from her mother—attempt to find a place for herself in impossible circumstances. Oprah said, "Her fiction is art—real, layered, and complex."

Classics

Anna Karenina
BY LEO TOLSTOY
Love, adultery, and loss are explored as the married heroine naively sacrifices her comfortable (and stifling) marriage for true love —only to find herself cut off from everything she knows.

A Tale of Two Cities, and Great Expectations
BY CHARLES DICKENS
Even if you read them in grade school, these iconic works are worth revisiting for their drama, character, and humanity.

Beginning and ending with some of English literature's most famous lines, *A Tale of Two Cities* has a sense of urgency and intimacy that draws you in. *Great Expectations*, about an orphan and the girl who beguiled him, is a sweeping story.

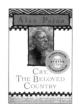

Cry, the Beloved Country
BY ALAN PATON
The saga of Stephen Kumalo—his struggle as a father, as a reverend, as a brother, and as a man— captures the very essence of South Africa in transition. It's a thought-provoking tragedy.

East of Eden
BY JOHN STEINBECK
Set in California's Salinas Valley, this multigenerational novel that draws on Biblical analogies tells the story of the Hamilton and Trask families and the bitter rivalries between brothers.

> "Stories have given me a place in which to lose myself."
>
> —ROXANE GAY

Light in August, The Sound and the Fury, and As I Lay Dying
BY WILLIAM FAULKNER

Oprah selected three Faulkner novels—Southern Gothic stories of men and women attempting to face loss and love and the shadows the past casts on the present.

One Hundred Years of Solitude
BY GABRIEL GARCÍA MÁRQUEZ

It's no secret the author loved telenovelas. This novel has all the makings of a drama—with a dash of magical realism. Three years after picking this, Oprah chose **Love in the Time of Cholera**, a love story that spans 50 years. Oprah said it's so beautifully written that it will make you ask yourself—how long could you, or would you, wait for love?

The Good Earth
BY PEARL S. BUCK

Awarded the Pulitzer Prize in 1932, it's a classic rags-to-riches story featuring a peasant Chinese farmer and the challenges faced once he attains wealth and influence.

The Heart Is a Lonely Hunter
BY CARSON MCCULLERS

The coming-of-age story pursues the themes of loneliness and isolation, with the racial disparity of the South serving as a backdrop.

Sula
BY TONI MORRISON

Set in a tight-knit neighborhood in Ohio known as "The Bottom," two Black girls are linked by a secret they've been harboring—a secret that ultimately follows them into adulthood and threatens their friendship.

Women's Stories

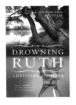

Drowning Ruth
BY CHRISTINA SCHWARZ
Love, loss, guilt, lies—these narrative strands run throughout this deftly woven story of three women and the shocking turn of events that changes their lives. Grippingly paced, it's a mesmerizing debut.

Gap Creek
BY ROBERT MORGAN
This bestseller features a badass woman who gets married soon after her brother's death while learning how to navigate adulthood.

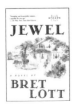

Jewel
BY BRET LOTT
Lott's novel follows the mother-daughter bond between Jewel and her last-born daughter, one that's drastically different from that with her other children.

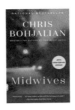

Midwives
BY CHRIS BOHJALIAN
After saving a child's life during an emergency C-section, Sibyl Danforth, a midwife, is wrapped into a sensational trial after being accused of accidentally killing the baby's mother in this riveting read.

Open House
BY ELIZABETH BERG
This features Samantha, a woman grappling with the aftermath of divorce while raising her 11-year-old son.

Songs in Ordinary Time
BY MARY MCGARRY MORRIS
In 1960 Vermont, a vulnerable divorcée falls prey to a con man in this masterful epic of the everyday, illuminating the compelling story of an unforgettable family.

Tara Road
BY MAEVE BINCHY

By a chance phone call, Ria meets Marilyn, a woman from New England unable to come to terms with her only son's death. The two women exchange houses for the summer with extraordinary consequences, each learning that the other has a deep secret that can never be revealed.

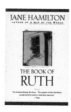

The Book of Ruth
BY JANE HAMILTON

The story of a woman coming to terms with her rocky relationship with her mother— and life alone—after her dad's death.

The Pilot's Wife
BY ANITA SHREVE

This novel recounts the story of a woman grappling with the death of her pilot husband—and the surprising revelations that come to light in the wake of a tragedy.

What Looks Like Crazy on an Ordinary Day
BY PEARL CLEAGE

Told through the lens of Ava Johnson, this story details what happens after a woman leaves the big city of Atlanta. For more than a decade, Ava had led a life of elegant, luxurious pleasures. But her fabulous career and her plans to achieve a powerful place were smashed to bits by one dark truth, sending her to a quieter, rural life back home.

While I Was Gone
BY SUE MILLER

Despite the fact that her life is seemingly picture-perfect, Jo Becker digs into her past after an appearance by a former housemate and faces the skeletons in her closet. It's a spellbinding novel of love and betrayal that explores what it means to be a good wife.

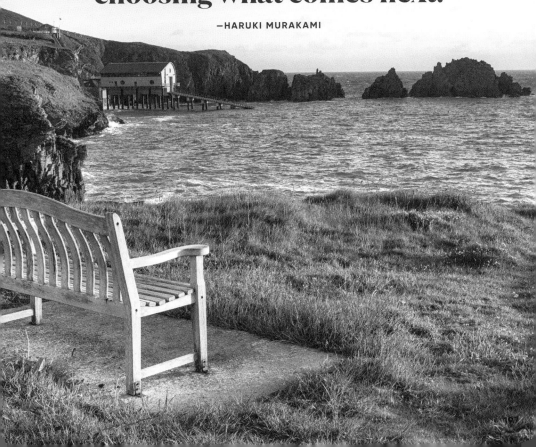

I'd like to hold on to that anticipation, the pleasure of choosing what comes next.

—HARUKI MURAKAMI

OPRAH'S FAVORITE FIRST SENTENCES

Some opening phrases stick with you forever.

"There's no way to know the exact second your life changes forever."

THE SUN DOES SHINE: HOW I FOUND LIFE AND FREEDOM ON DEATH ROW, BY ANTHONY RAY HINTON

"I spent much of my childhood listening to the sound of striving."

BECOMING, BY MICHELLE OBAMA

"Ruby Bell was a constant reminder of what could befall a woman whose standards were too high."

RUBY, BY CYNTHIA BOND

"On the morning of her ninth birthday, the day after Madame Françoise Derbanne slapped her, Suzette peed on the rosebushes."

CANE RIVER, BY LALITA TADEMY

"They shoot the white girl first. With the rest they can take their time."

PARADISE, BY TONI MORRISON

"First, I got myself born."

DEMON COPPERHEAD, BY BARBARA KINGSOLVER

"There was a time in Africa the people could fly."

THE INVENTION OF WINGS, BY SUE MONK KIDD

"All happy families are alike; each unhappy family is unhappy in its own way."

ANNA KARENINA, BY LEO TOLSTOY

"There are two kinds of people in the world, those who leave home, and those who don't."

AN AMERICAN MARRIAGE, BY TAYARI JONES

66

I consider reading a good book a sacred indulgence.

—OPRAH

MY "TO BE READ" LIST

It's the best of times (having just finished a great book) and the worst of times (figuring out what to read next!). So start a TBR list of possibilities—suggestions from friends, titles that got a great review, books everyone is talking about—and you'll always have something to look forward to.

TITLE	AUTHOR

TITLE	AUTHOR

MY HOPE IS this journal has helped you track your reading journey: books that took you to far-flung worlds and the ones that struck close to home. Books that sparked aha moments. Books that practically demanded to be shared with friends and family. Books that maybe even reconnected you with what it means to be human. You've gathered the quotes you wish to remember—and the writers you never want to forget. Not to mention lists with your next great read...and the one after that. From one reader to another, I wish you so many more blissful hours with a book at hand.

Oprah

Library of Congress Cataloging-in-Publication
Data Available on Request

10 9 8 7 6 5 4 3 2 1

HEARST
HOME

Published by Hearst Home, an imprint of Hearst Books/Hearst
Magazine Media, Inc.
300 W 57th Street
New York, NY 10019

FOUNDER AND EDITORIAL DIRECTOR, OPRAH DAILY: **Oprah Winfrey**
EDITOR AT LARGE, OPRAH DAILY: **Gayle King**
EDITORIAL DIRECTOR, OPRAH DAILY: **Pilar Guzmán**
CREATIVE DIRECTOR, OPRAH DAILY: **Adam Glassman**
CONTRIBUTING EDITOR AND WRITER: **M. D. Healey**
EDITORIAL DIRECTOR, OPRAH'S BOOK CLUB: **Leigh Newman**
DIRECTOR OF PHOTOGRAPHY: **Christina Weber**

VICE PRESIDENT, PUBLISHER, HEARST BOOKS: **Jacqueline Deval**
DEPUTY DIRECTOR, HEARST BOOKS: **Nicole Fisher**
CREATIVE DIRECTOR, HEARST PRODUCT STUDIO: **Gillian MacLeod**
DEPUTY MANAGING EDITOR, HEARST BOOKS: **Maria Ramroop**
SENIOR SALES & MARKETING COORDINATOR: **Nicole Plonski**

For information about custom editions,
special sales, premium and corporate purchases:
hearst.com/magazines/hearst-books

Printed in China
978-1-958395-17-2

"

I guess there are never enough books.

— JOHN STEINBECK

It's Your Time to Thrive!

Discover essential tools from Oprah Daily, including inspiring products and an all-access Oprah Insider membership, designed to help you manifest your goals and live your best life.